To:

From:

World's Best
Mother-in-Law

By Evelyn Loeb
and Virginia Reynolds

Peter Pauper Press, Inc.
WHITE PLAINS, NEW YORK

Designed by Taryn R. Sefecka
Illustrations copyright © 2004 Amy Dietrich

Copyright © 2004
Peter Pauper Press, Inc.
202 Mamaroneck Avenue
White Plains, NY 10601
All rights reserved
ISBN 0-88088-428-2
Printed in China
7 6 5 4 3 2 1

Visit us at www.peterpauper.com

World's Best
Mother-in-Law

When I got married, I never
imagined I'd get a wonderful
bonus—a terrific mother-in-law!
You've always been an undeniable
friend and confidant. The time has
come to say thank you, and give
credit where credit is deserved.
I hope this little book of loving
thoughts will let you know how
much you mean to me.

E. L. & V. R.

You can spell
"love" a thousand
different ways.

I couldn't have asked for a better mother-in-law if I created one myself!

Just like my
mother, you've
become a wonderful
role model to me.

You paved the
way for us, and
now we can make
our own journey.

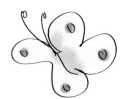

You encourage me
to go as far as my
dreams will take me.

You may let us
out of your sight,
but never out
of your heart.

You know
exactly when
to be nurse,
teacher,
cheerleader,
friend.

You'd feed the
world if you could,
and send everyone
home with leftovers.

As a good
mother-in-law, you do
a great balancing act
and make it look easy.

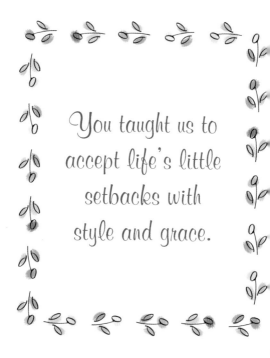

You taught us to accept life's little setbacks with style and grace.

You demonstrate
with all your
gestures that
"love is in the details."

You've turned
the refrigerator door
into a priceless art
gallery filled with your
grandchildren's
masterpieces.

You may disagree
with what we say,
but you'll defend our
right to say it.

I thank you for giving
me three invaluable gifts:
my spouse, my children,
and respect for the goals
I have set for myself.

You make
holidays magical
and turn ordinary
days into holidays.

You understand that the toughest part of being a good mother-in-law is knowing when to keep your mouth shut and your eyes closed.

You taught us all the important stuff—like how to spot a great bargain.

Your "restaurant"
is always open
(well, almost always).

You're always a
great source of support,
even when you're a
thousand miles away.

Your cookbook
is filled with recipes
for caring, warmth,
and compassion.

You wear so many
hats —mother-in-law,
wife, neighbor, friend—
and you wear them
so stylishly!

Why are there so many negative jokes about mothers-in-law? After all, you produced the person I love and adore!

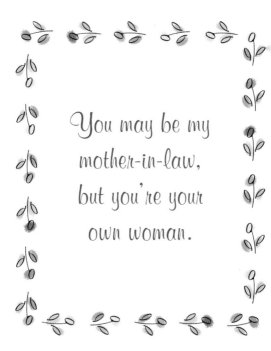

You may be my
mother-in-law,
but you're your
own woman.

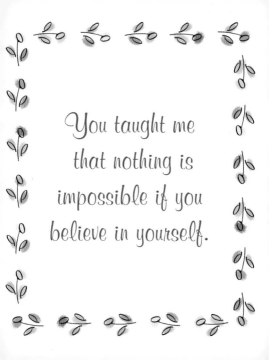

You taught me
that nothing is
impossible if you
believe in yourself.

Being there when needed
and when asked is probably
the best role you as a
mother-in-law can play.

A mother-in-law travels into uncharted waters every time one of her children marries.

Your love spreads
out like the branches of
a tree, sheltering what
grows beneath.

You can make even
a rainy day sparkle
with a smile.

Mother-in-law,
your values are an
anchor to steady us in
the roughest weather.

You taught us never
to dwell on our mistakes,
but to learn from them
and move on.

Mother-in-law, you've given us a lifetime of warm memories . . . with more to come!

When there wasn't enough candy for all, you claimed a sudden allergy to chocolate.

You are an integral
part of the loom on
which the tapestry
of our family is woven.

Your sweet
exterior conceals
a steely strength.

You know
how to use
laughter as a
healing balm.

Being a mother-in-law
is not for the
faint-hearted—and
I've never seen you faint!

You are a constant
reminder that the typical
mother-in-law jokes are
way off the mark.

How lucky I am!
You came along with
my true love as part of
a wonderful package.

Mother-in-law,
you never knew me as
a child—and that frees
me to be an adult with
you all the time.

You can be imitated,
but you can never
be duplicated.
You're one of a kind.

Thanks for
mothering me
whenever
I needed a lift.

You've been like
a mother to me.
Thanks for making
such a difference
in my life.

I'm thrilled to
be part of such
a unique, fun,
fabulous family.

You'd never let your child settle for second best—that's why I'm in the family!

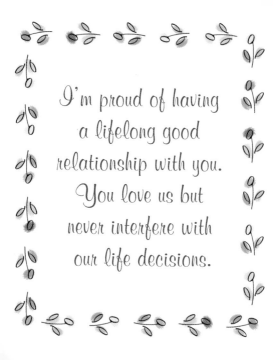

I'm proud of having
a lifelong good
relationship with you.
You love us but
never interfere with
our life decisions.

The fine example
you set will be
followed by your
children and
grandchildren, and
generations to follow.

Thanks to you,
my spouse's family
seems tailor-made—
just for me!

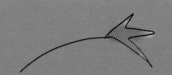

You know
the value of a kind
word, a smile, or a
compassionate silence.

You give everyone
in the family all
the necessary
room to grow.

I'm proud to pass
your traditions and
good genes down to my
own children.

Your marriage is an
ideal that my spouse and
I strive to emulate.

You know that it's more important to spend time with the grandchildren than it is to spend money on them.

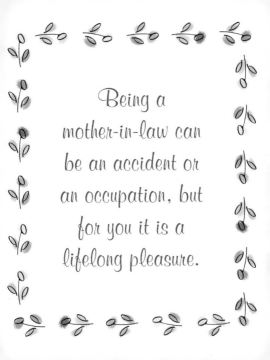

Being a
mother-in-law can
be an accident or
an occupation, but
for you it is a
lifelong pleasure.

You were my spouse's best coach and teacher. Now, you're mine, too!

One good
mother-in-law is
worth a hundred
marriage counselors.

You've lent a
sympathetic
shoulder when
my own strength
has faltered.

You delight in
our successes
and support us in
times of stress.

Together we can
laugh at ourselves,
and at each other!

Thanks for always
finding reasons
to celebrate!

You've always had a ready ear, which can be the most valuable of gifts.

How is it that
you're so busy,
and yet you always
have time for me?

Like the dearest
of friends, you
respond without
being called.

Happiness is
contagious, and
you make sure
we get our
daily dose!

Thank you for
accepting affection
with open arms
and giving it with
an open heart.

You've helped teach
me that relationships
are like precious gems:
if we treasure them,
they will sparkle.

I'm so proud to
have you as my
mother-in-law, and
so grateful for the
times we have together.